3X 2/10✓ 4/10

PIERS AND OTHER
SEASIDE ARCHITECTURE

Lynn F Pearson

D0033384

3 1336 08252 5602

SAN DIEGO PUBLIC
LIBRARY
LA JOLLA

SHIRE PUBLICATIONS

SEP 10 2009

First published in Great Britain in 2002; second edition
2008 by Shire Publications Ltd, Midland House, West Way,
Botley, Oxford OX2 0PH, United Kingdom.
443 Park Avenue South, New York, NY 10016, USA.

E-mail: shire@shirebooks.co.uk   www.shirebooks.co.uk

© 2002 and 2008 Lynn F. Pearson

All rights reserved. Apart from any fair dealing for the
purpose of private study, research, criticism or review, as
permitted under the Copyright, Designs and Patents Act,
1988, no part of this publication may be reproduced,
stored in a retrieval system, or transmitted in any form or
by any means, electronic, electrical, chemical, mechanical,
optical, photocopying, recording or otherwise, without the
prior written permission of the copyright owner.
Enquiries should be addressed to the Publishers.

Every attempt has been made by the publisher to secure
the appropriate permissions for materials reproduced in
this book. If there has been any oversight we will be happy
to rectify the situation and a written submission should be
made to the Publishers.

A CIP catalogue record for this book is available from the
British Library.

Shire Library no. 406   •   ISBN-13: 978 0 7478 0693 6

Lynn F. Pearson has asserted her right under the
Copyright, Designs and Patents Act, 1988,
to be identified as the author of this book.

Designed by Ken Vail Graphic Design, Cambridge, UK and
typeset in Perpetua and Gill Sans.
Printed in Malta by Gutenberg Press Ltd.

08 09 10 11 12   10 9 8 7 6 5 4 3 2 1

COVER IMAGE

A train on Southend Pier approaches one of the pier's
shelters. The pier, built from rolled steel joists (horizontal
members) on cast-iron screw piles, is now served by
lightweight electric trains running on 3-foot gauge tracks,
the single-track railway being completely separated from
the footway.

TITLE PAGE IMAGE

Bangor Garth Pier opened in 1896. It was built using cast-
iron columns and screw piles, with wrought iron and steel
for other structural members; it reaches two-thirds of the
way across the Menai Strait. The ornamental ironwork and
series of kiosks dotted along its 1,550-foot length give it
the appearance of an early Victorian pier.

CONTENTS PAGE IMAGE

Great Yarmouth Britannia Pier's first permanent pavilion, a
triumph of prefabrication, which opened in June 1902.
The pier itself was the second on the site; the original
700-foot-long Britannia Pier was built in 1857–8 but
demolished after the 1899 summer season and replaced
with a slightly longer pier, which opened in 1901. The
second pier's designers were the Manchester brothers
James and Arthur Mayoh, the contractors being their firm
Mayoh & Haley.

ACKNOWLEDGEMENTS

The author is very grateful to the following for their
assistance, in many and various ways, with this book: Penny
Beckett, Lisa Dearnley-Davison, Martin Easdown, Gwyn
and Marie Evans, John Garlick, Tony and Kathy Herbert,
Sue Hudson, Steve Hunt, Biddy Macfarlane, Geoff Maggs,
Ian McChesney, Sophie Murray, Chris and Mick Paxton,
Jim and Margaret Perry, Peter Revell, John Rotheroe,
Derek Sugden, Jane Webb, Mark Whyman, Blackpool
Borough Council, Blackpool Pleasure Beach, the Friends of
the Midland Hotel, the Museum of London, the National
Piers Society, Southern Water, Spence Associates and the
Tiles and Architectural Ceramics Society.

Illustrations are acknowledged as follows: courtesy of
Rebecca Bingham, page 40 (top); courtesy of Blackpool
Pleasure Beach, page 40 (bottom); courtesy of Russell
Butcher, page 57 (top); courtesy of Lisa Dearnley-Davison,
page 24 (left), 57 (bottom left); courtesy of Tony Herbert,
46 (right); courtesy of Cadbury Lamb, page 9 (upper
middle); courtesy of the Marlinova Collection, page 30, 36
(top); courtesy of the Museum of London, page 23 (top);
courtesy of Southern Water, page 54 (bottom), 55 (top);
courtesy of Andy Stagg, page 49 (bottom); courtesy of
P. L. Watson, Delattre Photographique, page 29; author's
collection, pages 3, 7 (top middle), 12 (top), 15 (bottom
left), 16 (bottom), 17 (bottom), 19 (top), 32, 34 (right),
35 (top), 37. All other photographs were taken by the
author.

Shire Publications is supporting the Woodland Trust, the UK's leading woodland conservation charity, by funding the dedication of trees.

CONTENTS

PLEASURE PIERS AND PAVILIONS   5

MODERN PIERS   21

THE PEOPLE'S PLEASURE PALACES   31

ENTERTAINMENT ASHORE   39

LIVING AND WORKING AT THE SEASIDE   51

FURTHER READING   58

PLACES TO VISIT   60

INDEX   64

PLEASURE PIERS AND PAVILIONS

THE concept of the pleasure pier originated out of the sheer difficulty of reaching the seaside watering places that had become popular during the late eighteenth and early nineteenth centuries.

Prospective visitors initially had the choice of expensive stagecoaches or slow sailing-boats, but the introduction of quick, reliable steam passenger vessels around 1815 transformed the journey to nascent resorts such as Weymouth and Margate. There remained, however, the problem of transferring passengers from ship to shore where docking facilities were inadequate. Travelling to the Isle of Wight by ship to Ryde involved a long walk across a wet, sandy beach when arriving at low tide. This was seen by the townspeople as a deterrent to visitors, and a landing pier was built in 1813–14. Although little more than a long, narrow wooden jetty – it was 1,740 feet in length but only 12 feet wide – and completely bereft of any decorative features, the pier was so successful that it was repeatedly extended and the pierhead enlarged during the following two decades.

As with the piers built at Brighton, Leith, Southend, Walton on the Naze, Herne Bay, Southampton and Deal during the 1820s and 1830s, landing charges for goods and passengers provided the income for Ryde Pier, but during the 1840s it became obvious that piers were also being used for reasons other than the purely functional. Visitors, attracted to the sea but repelled by its danger, could promenade along the pier in complete safety and still enjoy a frisson of excitement caused by the proximity of the waves below.

The noise of the sea, the therapeutic sea breeze, the activities on the landing-stage, the view of ships and shore, all made the pier a unique resort attraction, and one that could clearly be made more profitable, particularly as the expansion of the railway network during the 1840s and 1850s brought the seaside within easy reach of many more people than before. The addition of a toll-house, turnstiles, or both, at the shore end of the pier allowed a charge to be made for promenading, either daily or by means of a season ticket. A classical toll-house was installed at the entrance to Ryde Pier before

Opposite: Before its development as a resort from the 1850s, Llandudno had been little more than a hamlet lying between the Great Orme and Little Orme headlands. The Mostyn Estate built wide promenades and impressive terraces, while the pier was erected by the Llandudno Pier Company in 1876–7. The contractor was John Dixon, a railway builder who had been responsible for shipping Cleopatra's Needle to England and had worked with James Brunlees on Southport Pier, perfecting the jetting system of construction.

Top: Saltburn Pier was designed by John Anderson and opened in 1869; a bandstand was added to the pierhead in 1885 but lost after a ship collided with the pier in 1924. The entrance buildings date from the latter part of the 1920s. The pier was breached for defence purposes during the Second World War, then rebuilt in 1947.

Right: Although it lost its 1895 pavilion in 1971, Ryde Pier on the Isle of Wight remains an excellent promenading pier with abundant cast ironwork; the balustrade dates from around 1880. It continues to handle ferry passenger traffic across the Solent, and trains still depart from the pierhead. Ryde Victoria Pier, which stood about 500 yards to the east, was built in 1864 to be used by a ferry service, but eventually became a bathing station. These facilities fell into disuse around the turn of the century, and the pier was demolished around 1916, with the last traces being washed away in 1924.

1840, and later piers utilised picturesque or oriental styles for these small but significant structures.

Facilities for promenaders slowly improved: a further pavilion was added to Ryde Pier in 1842, while the 200-foot length of the Royal Terrace Pier (1843–5) at Milton-on-Thames, near Gravesend, was both illuminated and covered. Great Yarmouth's Wellington Pier (1853) included a promenading platform at its seaward end, and Southport Pier (1859–60) was built primarily as a promenading pier, although much of its success resulted from its position on a regular paddle-steamer route.

Southport was also unusual because of its building method, which avoided pile-driving. In contrast to harbour piers, which were normally built from solid masonry, seaside piers were generally constructed of piles connected by a lattice framework; this was cheaper than masonry and less resistant to water movement. A seaside pier usually comprised upright piles, girders connecting the piles at their top ends, decking above the horizontal girders, and struts and bracing members linking the previous three. Initially, piers were built wholly of timber, the piles being driven into the seabed by piling engines,

Left: Herne Bay's first pier – a 3,633-foot-long landing stage – opened in 1832, but damage by Teredo worm led to its demolition in 1870. The second pier, a short structure intended for promenading, opened in 1873 but was almost completely rebuilt during 1896–9; its new length of 3,787 feet made it the second longest pier in Britain. The postcard shows the Grand Pavilion (1910) to the rear of the entrance buildings; it was destroyed by fire in 1970 and a leisure centre opened in its place in 1976. Just visible at the pier's seaward end is a tiny pavilion.

Right: The Wellington Pier Gardens in Great Yarmouth were centred upon the ornate bandstand, with the Winter Gardens (left) to the north, an arcade and the pier itself to the east, and much use of decorative pinky-red terracotta balustrading to define the sunken garden space beside Marine Parade. Some of the terracotta work bears the town's coat of arms. Wellington Pier is seen here complete with its original detailing, well before its re-cladding in the 1950s.

but engineers found that the timbers were attacked by marine worms and borers and so from the mid 1840s began to use cast-iron piles. At first the piles were square in cross-section but these were soon replaced with circular castings, which offered less water resistance, and the invention of screw piles provided a further improvement. Screw piles, fitted with blades enabling them to be screwed directly into the ground, were first used at Margate Pier (1853–7) by the civil engineer Eugenius Birch (1818–84), the foremost of the Victorian pier designers. Neither screw nor driven piles were used for

Bangor Garth Pier was designed by the engineer John James Webster and built by the contractor Alfred Thorne; the same combination successfully completed the construction of a pier at Dover in 1893. The design of Bangor's promenading pier is enlivened by oriental-style toll-houses and kiosks, the latter supported on braced towers at intervals of 250 feet.

Above: Every iron column at Colwyn Bay Victoria Pier is stamped with the ironfounders' name – the Widnes Foundry Company – and an individual column number; the decorative capitals support a horizontal lattice girder. The Widnes Foundry Company also supplied ironwork for Morecambe West End Pier (1893–6), Mumbles Pier (1897–8) and Great Yarmouth Britannia Pier (1900–1).

Top left: Southport Pier, opened in 1860, was one of the earliest pleasure piers. Its maximum length after extensions during the 1860s was 4,380 feet, but damage by storm and fire has reduced this to 3,633 feet, still making Southport the second-longest pier in Britain after Southend. The pier was threatened with demolition in the early 1990s but its restoration was completed in 2002 with the opening of a new pavilion at the pierhead.

Top right: Colwyn Bay Victoria Pier was designed by the specialist seaside architects Mangnall & Littlewoods of Manchester and built in 1899–1900. The prefabricated iron substructure carried a 2,500-seat pavilion, which burned down in 1922. Its replacement was also destroyed by fire in 1933, although another pavilion opened the following year. The pier has been under threat of closure or demolition since the 1970s; although it reopened in 1995, further restoration is still required.

Southport and its two 1860s extensions, but a method known as jetting, in which water was pumped down through a tube within the pile, agitating the sand beneath and allowing the pile to sink into place.

Initially, timber was used for the horizontal members, but this was soon replaced by wrought iron, its torsional strength making it better suited for this purpose than cast iron; cheap steel replaced wrought iron in the late nineteenth century. Girders tended to be either solid I-section or latticework in varying formats; the latter were lighter and were inherently decorative. Along with lattice girders, different arrangements of columns and struts (taking compression) and ties (in tension) could result in a highly ornate and elegant substructure. The delicate, curving ironwork of Clevedon Pier (1867–9) is the most memorable in this respect, but the complex system of

The Pavilion Theatre, at the landward end of Weymouth's Pleasure Pier, was built in 1908. It was a mostly wooden structure with a steel frame, the design being the winning entry in a 1907 architectural competition. The Pavilion closed during the Second World War, reopened in 1950 as the Ritz Theatre, but burnt down – in little more than an hour – on 13 April 1954 during refurbishment. Its replacement, the new Pavilion Theatre, opened in 1960, but the entire area is due to be redeveloped, with detailed plans being submitted in 2008.

THE PAVILION, WEYMOUTH.

Clevedon Pier's eight arches, each spanning 100 feet, were created using Barlow rails, a patent wrought-iron rail section, riveted to curved iron flats. The pier opened in 1869 and the pavilion, by Milton Iron Works, was added in 1894. To accommodate the wide tidal range (up to 49 feet), flights of steps ran up through the pierhead so that passengers could alight at any state of the tide.

Birnbeck Pier (1864–7) at Weston-super-Mare links the mainland with rocky Birnbeck Island, then continues out into the Bristol Channel with a 250-foot wooden landing-stage added in 1872. The pier was lit by gas lamps and was immediately popular, with 120,000 people paying the one penny admission charge in the first three months. A pavilion was added to the pier in 1884.

Eugenius Birch worked with the Glasgow contractor Robert Laidlaw on the construction of Blackpool North Pier (1862–3), and the pair went on to build piers at Brighton (West), Deal, Lytham and Hastings. The North Pier's tiny kiosks were part of an ornate design that included intricate wrought ironwork forming continuous seating along the pier sides.

Sandown Pier, on
the Isle of Wight,
opened in 1879; its
extension, including
a seaward-end
pavilion, opened in
1895, and a shore-
end pavilion was
added in 1934.
Between 1968 and
1973 the pier was
rebuilt; the seaward-
end pavilion was
demolished, a new
Pavilion Theatre was
added, many of the
iron piles were
replaced with
concrete and much
of the decking was
renewed. Although
the Pavilion remains
intact, the theatre
ceased to operate in
1997.

angled bracing used by Birch at Weston-super-Mare's Birnbeck Pier (1864–7)
is also very attractive. Decking was normally made of wood, the timbers
often being laid herring-bone style and cambered.

The piers of the 1860s were transitional, being neither mere landing-stages
nor pure pleasure piers; their architects tentatively embarked on the addition
of decorative features designed to pull in the potential crowds. Two piers
designed by Eugenius Birch included a series of substantial kiosks along the
length of the pier: at Blackpool North (1862–3) these were Italianate in style,
while in Brighton Birch took his lead from the Royal Pavilion (which had
been transformed into an exotic domed palace for the Prince Regent in
1815–23) and selected an oriental theme for the West Pier (1863–6).

Shops, first seen as an addition to Brighton's Chain Pier (1822–3) in the
1830s, reappeared on Rhyl Pier (1867) along with a restaurant and a bandstand,
while the Birch-designed New Brighton Pier (1866–7) in the Wirral featured
restaurants and a central saloon with an observation tower. A few of the longer
piers also incorporated passenger railways, some of which began as the
contractors' own lines, with propulsion originally provided by hand or horse.
Southport's cable-operated passenger tramway opened in 1865.

It was still the case that sixteen of the twenty-two piers begun during the
1860s were plain landing-stages with the minimum of buildings. Placing
more emphasis on pier entertainment required the companies that
promoted pier building to put up increased capital, although with the

The cast-iron base of a lamp standard on Clevedon Pier showing the name of
the contractor, Hamilton's Windsor Iron Works of Liverpool, and the date
1868. The panel on the left of the base carries the names of the pier's designers
and engineers, John William Grover (1836–92) and Richard J. Ward (1817–81) of
London. Amongst many other works, Grover had also been responsible for the design
of the dome for the 1862 International Exhibition building in London.

incentive of enhanced financial returns from promenaders spending extra time and money on the pier.

Promoting a pier was not without its drawbacks. Consent for the construction of a pier had to be obtained from Parliament by means of a parliamentary bill, and from the foreshore authority, which was often the Board of Trade but which could involve local lords of the manor and other bodies. Once consent had been obtained, building took place in an environment surpassed in difficulty only by the construction of rock lighthouses and, even when the pier was complete, the unique combination of dangers from waves, wind, fire and collision led to the loss of many pier pavilions and sections of pier. Of course, not all proposals for piers resulted in a successful conclusion: Lowestoft New Pier (1899), intended to extend from Britain's most easterly point, was never built, while the delightfully domed Whitley Bay Pier (1908) reached the design stage but no further and the resort remained pierless.

Finance for pier promotion might be obtained from local residents and businesses, or regionally, often from urban centres in the catchment area of the resort, or sometimes nationally. The most common means of raising capital was via the joint stock company, which could be formed by a minimum of seven people, but it was the advent of limited liability (following law changes after 1855) that led to a boom in small share ownership, and many more resort-based pier and entertainment companies were formed from the 1860s onward.

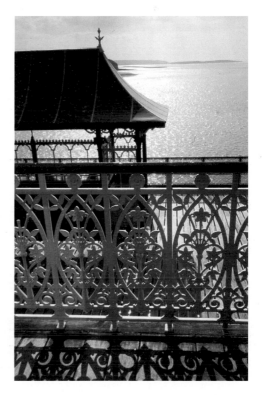

The pier that heralded the exuberant superstructure of pavilions and kiosks now associated with the Victorian and Edwardian seaside was Hastings Pier (1869–72), which was the first to have a substantial pavilion (with accommodation for 2,000 people) included as an integral part of the original plan.

Ornate ironwork on the first floor balcony of the 1894 pavilion at the seaward end of Clevedon Pier. The cast-iron pavilion and the twin pierhead shelters were constructed by architectural ironwork specialists McDowall Steven & Co of Glasgow's Milton Ironworks, under the supervision of the Town Surveyor. The original wooden pierhead had itself been replaced by a cast-iron structure in 1892–3.

Eugenius Birch included this domed and arcaded seaward-end 2,000-seat pavilion in his original design for the 910-foot Hastings Pier. The pavilion was burnt out in 1917 and replaced by a less elaborate structure in 1922. The pier's substructure comprises cast-iron columns on screw piles with lattice girders above.

Both pier and oriental-style pavilion were designed by Eugenius Birch, who built a total of fourteen piers in England and Wales, seven of which survive: Aberystwyth, Blackpool North, Bournemouth, Brighton West, Eastbourne, Hastings and Weston-super-Mare (Birnbeck). His pioneering use of the oriental style during the 1860s instigated its revival, and it eventually became the archetypal English seaside architectural style. Birch's huge contribution to the seaside included the first recreational aquarium (Brighton, 1872) and Scarborough Aquarium (1877), the latter being an extravagantly decorative Indo-Moorish structure, which was demolished in 1968 to make way for a car park.

Another notable pier designer was Sir James Brunlees (1816–92), a civil engineer who generally worked on railways and docks. He used the unusual water-jetting system to construct Southport Pier and was also responsible for the piers at Llandudno (1876–7) and Rhyl (1867); he built the second Southend Pier in 1888–90. Joseph William Wilson (1829–98), an engineer who had worked on the Crystal Palace, built four piers during 1864–73:

Aberystwyth Royal Pier (1864–5) was built by Eugenius Birch and the contractor J. E. Dowson, with whom Birch also worked on New Brighton, Eastbourne and Scarborough piers. Dowson died in the late 1860s before the last two were completed and the Stockton firm Head Wrightson took over the contracts. The Aberystwyth pavilion dates from 1896; in the distance is the cliff railway, which opened in the same year.

Below: Llandudno Pier is notable for the fact that it is a dog-leg in plan rather than straight, and for its lavish use of ornamental wrought and cast ironwork in balustrades and railings. Each of the octagonal kiosks has ironwork of unusual design beneath its overhanging roof.

Above: Elegantly curved ironwork seating at Eastbourne Pier. The width of the pier's neck is 27 feet, and it is built on cast-iron screw piles supported by specially made cups resting on bedrock below the sand. This arrangement allows the pier some movement during bad weather.

The ironwork of the railings at Colwyn Bay's Victoria Pier, supplied by the Widnes Foundry Company, carries the logo of the Victoria Pier Company. Restoration of the pier is estimated to cost in the region of £4 million, and would include repairs to the pier's structure, renovation of the 1933–4 pavilion – which may still retain its tea room murals by Eric Ravilious, hidden beneath later cladding – and the construction of several small buildings providing essential commercial space.

One mile from the shore along Southend Pier, and still another 1,800 feet to go to the pier head. The alternative to walking the planks is a ride on the pier trains, now a diesel-operated service running on 3-foot-gauge track; there is a single line with a passing loop. One train is named after Sir John Betjeman (1906–84), the first honorary president of the National Piers Society, which was founded in 1979.

Bognor Regis, Teignmouth, Westward Ho! and Hunstanton. John James Webster (1845–1914), an engineer who specialised in bridge construction, designed piers at Dover, Bangor and Minehead in 1892–1901.

As pier and pavilion design required a combination of engineering and design skills, it was not surprising that many firms, including engineers, general contractors, ironfounders and prefabrication specialists, became involved in the process, along with architects whose practices happened to be based at resorts or in their catchment areas. The seaside became a profitable arena for the ironfounders, whose catalogues provided much of the decorative pier furniture as well as the substructure. Boulton & Paul of Norwich, specialists in prefabricated timber-and-iron structures,

Bangor Garth Pier suffered collision damage in 1914, with permanent repairs and improvements finally being made in 1921 when it was found that the central piles had settled 4.5 inches. The pier closed in 1971 for safety reasons but was re-opened after restoration in 1988. The curved ironwork that forms seating along the sides of the pier is especially elegant.

Right: Head Wrightson were contractors for Cleethorpes Pier, erecting the iron piling, with its decorative capitals, and the unusual arched ironwork spans. The shore-end pavilion dates from 1905 and – although much altered – still retains its original roof structure.

Right: Cromer Pier (1900–1) stands directly below the Hotel de Paris, built (around existing properties) in 1895–6 by the Norwich architect George Skipper (1856–1948). He designed two other massive hotels at the little resort, the Grand (1890–1) and the Metropole (1893–4), but both were demolished in the 1970s.

Southsea's Clarence Pier was built in 1860–1, the pavilion being added in 1882; the stubby pier's width is greater than its length. The resort's second pier, South Parade, was constructed during 1875–8 by Head Wrightson and opened in 1879. A fire in 1904 resulted in a complete rebuilding, which took until 1908.

Clacton Pier's oval-plan seaward-end pavilion was built in 1893, the curving ironwork of its structure still visible following storm damage to later cladding. The pavilion was designed as a concert hall. A shore-end pavilion, the Ocean Theatre, was added in 1928, followed by the Crystal Casino in 1932 (demolished in 1940).

Above left: Looking shoreward on Southend Pier, Britain's longest pier at 7,080 feet and nearly twice as long as Southport Pier, the second longest. The first pier at Southend opened in 1830 and was extended to become the longest pier in Europe by 1846. The present pier is based on the iron pier built in 1888–90 by James Brunlees.

Above right: All that remains of the winter-garden-style pavilion (1883–4) at Llandudno Pier is a series of ironwork columns still carrying their decorative spandrels and the iron stairs reaching to the sky. The pavilion, which was a 2,000-seat theatre with a cast-iron veranda on the seaward side, was repaired during the 1980s but was empty from 1990; a 1994 fire brought about its demolition.

illustrated a substantial pavilion as supplied to clients at Scheveningen, on the Dutch coast, in their 1898 catalogue and provided a larger version in 1902 for Great Yarmouth's Britannia Pier. It was probably the largest of the prefabricated pier buildings until it was destroyed by fire in 1909.

After the pier-construction boom of the 1860s and 1870s, when an average of two new piers per year appeared on the British coastline, pier development in the final quarter of the nineteenth century concentrated upon the pavilions, which were transformed from functional shelters to ornate palaces of entertainment. They were an eclectic bunch in architectural terms, ranging from Birch's stunning Indian Pavilion on Blackpool North Pier (1874, destroyed by fire in 1921) to Llandudno's shore-end iron-and-glass winter garden (1883–4, demolished after a fire in 1994) and the Arts-and-Crafts-style cottage on Lowestoft's South Pier (1891, demolished in the late 1940s). During the 1890s and early 1900s a series of huge marine palaces, mostly oriental in style, was built on the piers of Sussex and Lancashire, the most spectacular being the 'Taj Mahal of the North' added to Morecambe Central Pier in 1897; it was the work of specialist seaside architects Mangnall &

The pavilion known as the 'Taj Mahal of the North' was added to Morecambe Central Pier in 1897. It was built by the Morecambe Pier and Pavilion Company to enable their pier – which opened in 1869 and had few entertainment facilities – to compete with the town's new West End Pier, which was not only much longer but came equipped with a seaward-end pavilion.

Littlewoods of Manchester. The most unusual pavilion of this era was designed by Great Yarmouth's borough surveyor J. W. 'Concrete' Cockrill for the town's Wellington Pier in 1903. Its idiosyncratic clean-cut modern style was reminiscent of contemporary exhibition buildings. Its decorative finials were lost when the pavilion was re-clad in the 1950s, and the entire – by then rather neglected – pavilion was taken down by Great Yarmouth Borough Council in 2005–6, the intention being to replace it with an entertainment centre having a similar appearance to the original pavilion; this was under construction in 2008.

Although nine piers were completed during the first decade of the twentieth century, eight of these opened between 1901 and 1905, with Weston-super-Mare Grand Pier (1904), complete with an integral 2,000-seat pavilion, being the most impressive. Fleetwood Pier (1910), only 492 feet long, and Burnham-on-Sea Pier (1911), an even shorter structure built from concrete, were the last pleasure piers to be built before the Second World War. Pavilions, however, continued to be added to existing piers. Most were small domed or barrel-vaulted halls with little decoration, or even

Above left: Blackpool Tower seen from beneath the Central Pier, with the North Pier in the distance. The Central (originally South) Pier was built in 1867–8 by the contractor Robert Laidlaw; its iron columns were placed at 60-foot intervals and linked by wrought-iron girders. The pier was always renowned for its popular entertainments.

Above right: Lowestoft's Claremont Pier was 600 feet long and used by steamers when it was built in 1902–3. The last steamer called in 1939 and the pier was derelict by 1948, although a new shore-end pavilion was built shortly afterwards. Restoration of the pavilion began in 1988, and a colourful (and successful) beach-hut promenade development was introduced just to the south in the late 1990s.

The 1,800-foot-long Morecambe West End Pier (1893–6) was built by the contractors Mayoh & Haley with prefabricated iron parts supplied by the Widnes Foundry Company. The large domed pavilion, an integral part of the original design, was destroyed by fire in 1917; the pier itself was demolished in 1978.

Above left: In Great
Yarmouth, Wellington
Pier's pavilion, originally
clad in metallic Uralite,
was still a striking and
unusual structure until
its demolition in 2005–6.
Its architect, John
William Cockrill
(1849–1924), was
particularly interested
in building with
ceramics and concrete,
even attempting to
persuade property
owners to concrete
over Yarmouth's narrow
lanes (known as rows).
This earned him the
nickname 'Concrete'
Cockrill.

prefabricated structures, but there were exceptions: a Moorish-style
pavilion was added to the pier at St Anne's-on-the-Sea in 1904, while
Brighton West Pier's Concert Hall (1914–16), its delicate ironwork
engineered by Noel Ridley, could seat up to 1,400 people. This pavilion
was the home of the West Pier Orchestra, although its floor could be
cleared to host other activities such as roller-skating or ballroom dancing.
The range of activities available on piers, which by the early twentieth
century included music and shows (everything from German bands and
minstrels to pantomime, opera and music hall), aquatic performances and
slot-machines, expanded still further after the First World War to take in
fairground rides, cinemas, vast dance halls, sunbathing and sophisticated
amusement arcades. The piers of the 1920s and 1930s were just as popular
as those of the late nineteenth century.

Funding for pier improvements increasingly came from local councils,
anxious to promote tourism. Great Yarmouth council bought the town's
Wellington Pier in 1900, funding its reconstruction and the addition of a
new pavilion as well as the transport of a winter garden from Torquay to add

Above right: Weston-
super-Mare's Grade II
listed Grand Pier, seen
here before its massive
pavilion (1932–3) was
destroyed by fire on 28
July 2008. It was a
replacement for the
original pavilion, which
burned down in 1930.
The pier itself is an
iron-piled structure
erected by the
contractors Mayoh &
Haley; its framework of
lattice girders is carried
by cast-iron columns
grouped in tens.

Brighton West Pier's first great
pavilion (right) was constructed
at its seaward end in 1893 by
the engineer Peregrine Birch
(1845–96), son of Eugenius
Birch, builder of the West Pier.
Brighton Corporation forced
the removal of a large dome
from the younger Birch's
pavilion design. The Concert
Hall (left) was designed by
Clayton & Black and added in
1914–16, its completion being
delayed by the war. The interior
featured coloured designs
stencilled on the walls.

Morecambe Central Pier's exotic Indian-style pavilion was destroyed by fire in 1933; a 2,000-seat replacement pavilion-cum-ballroom was put up in 1935–6. The pier closed in 1986 after partial collapse of its decking; then the pavilion was burnt down in 1991; complete demolition of the pier followed in 1992. It had at least outlasted the rival West End Pier by well over a decade.

to the entertainment complex. In Worthing, the corporation bought the pier in 1920, repaired it and provided it with a shore-end concert pavilion in 1925–6 at a total cost of almost £60,000; the borough architect designed its highly glazed modernist, metal-clad seaward-end pavilion in 1935. Financial difficulties suffered by pier-building companies often necessitated the involvement of local councils; continued deterioration of the fabric of Victorian piers and pavilions meant resorts were left without their most attractive amenities.

Several pavilions fell victim to fire, notably Birch's Indian Pavilion at Blackpool North Pier (1921) and the 'Taj Mahal of the North' on Morecambe Central Pier (1933). Great Yarmouth's unlucky Britannia Pier suffered a series of fires, beginning in 1909 with the destruction of the first pavilion (1902). The second pavilion (1910) was burnt out in 1914 and the Floral Hall Ballroom (1928) followed in 1932. During a fire in 1954 its replacement, the Grand Ballroom (1933), perished, as did the third pavilion in 1914. By 1939, although 101 pleasure piers had been erected, twenty-five had already been demolished or rebuilt, leaving seventy-six to face the rigours of the coming war.

Looking south along the beach at Great Yarmouth towards the Wellington Pier and Winter Gardens, before demolition of the pier pavilion in 2005–6. The Winter Gardens, which opened at Torquay in 1881, was designed by local architects John Watson and William Harvey, while the ironwork was supplied by the Crescent Iron Works of Willenhall. It was never successful and was bought by Great Yarmouth council in 1903 for £1,300, dismantled, shipped round the coast and re-erected. It enjoyed happier times in Yarmouth, which prospered in the Edwardian era.

MODERN PIERS

THE Second World War was especially disastrous for piers on the south and east coasts, many of which were breached to prevent their use as landing-stages; floating mines and enemy action also caused damage. A worse fate befell Minehead Pier, built in 1900–1, which was completely demolished in 1940 to provide nearby gun batteries with a clear line of sight; in the same year, Deal Pier was taken down following a ship collision. After the end of the war the remaining piers, tattered and broken, were returned to their owners. Some financial compensation was available, but eight piers were eventually lost during the 1950s, mainly as an indirect result of combined wartime and storm damage, including St Leonards Palace Pier (1888–91) with its fine oriental-flavour pavilion. Here, breaching, bombs and fire had severely affected the pier's structure, and demolition followed further gale damage in 1951.

Many piers were rapidly reconstructed and were able to reopen soon after the war ended, although structural damage to others resulted in considerable cuts in their deck length. At Deal a completely new pier was built in 1954–7 with reinforced concrete, a material that had been used for pier repairs since the mid 1920s. The design, by Sir William Halcrow and Partners, comprised concrete decking above slightly inclined piles; although traditional in plan, the effect was wholly modern and very unlike the eccentric, colourful architecture of the 1951 Festival of Britain, which included the Seaside Pavilion, part of which was intended to resemble a pier. Deal was the sole new pleasure pier to be erected in the second half of the twentieth century, although the continued popularity of the British seaside holiday during the 1950s led to the construction of some new pavilions whose design was rather different from that of their predecessors, for instance Lowestoft South Pier's glass-walled stairwell topped by an observation platform.

During the 1960s and 1970s, before appreciation of the delights of Victorian architecture became widespread, another eight piers were demolished. Only fifty-nine piers remained when the National Piers Society was founded in 1979, its aims being to promote and sustain interest in the preservation and enjoyment of seaside piers. The destruction of Redcar Pier

Opposite: Cromer Pier opened in 1901, replacing two earlier jetties, both of which had been washed away by heavy seas. The seaward end was extended in 1905 when the pavilion was built; this still functions as a traditional summer-season variety theatre.

The no-frills concrete structure of Deal Pier, which reaches out 1,026 feet into the English Channel. The pier, which cost £250,000 and was opened by the Duke of Edinburgh in 1957, is basically a promenade pier with fishing facilities.

in 1981 – sold off for just £250 – seemed to signal a decade in which pier restoration was greeted with enthusiasm by the public and became acceptable to funding bodies. Bangor Garth Pier, closed in 1971 and threatened with demolition, was restored during 1982–8, while Clevedon Pier (now Grade I listed) reopened in 1989 after almost two decades of fund-raising and rebuilding, although its full restoration was completed only in 1998, when Swanage and Penarth Piers were also reopened following renovation.

Eastbourne Pier was designed by Eugenius Birch and opened on 13 June 1870, although work was not finally completed until 1872. A small seaward-end theatre was added in 1888 and replaced by a larger structure in 1899–1901 that included a dome containing a camera obscura. The 1901 theatre was badly damaged by fire in 1970, and the building was then converted to a nightclub. A 900-seat pavilion built at the shoreward end in 1925 later became an amusement arcade, and the camera obscura – in its dome above the nightclub – was reopened to the public in 2003. Eastbourne Pier is listed Grade II and retains much of its Victorian charm.

Above: The 'Seaside Pavilion' at the Festival of Britain, drawn by the artist Bryan de Grineau and reproduced in the *Illustrated London News* of 26 May 1951. Visitors on the left can be seen looking out over the Thames from a pier-like structure supported by lattice girders. The pavilion, designed by Eric Brown and Peter Chamberlin, also included rock making, saucy postcards and donkey rides, all intended to represent the 'essentially English' seaside.

The new entrance to Southend Pier was designed by Emptage Architects of Ingatestone in Essex and opened in summer 2003. The RNLI Lifeboat Station at the pierhead opened in 2002, along with a newly built north slipway, replacing the one destroyed in the July 1976 fire. Another fire, on 9 October 2005, badly damaged the pierhead, but the pier reopened in August 2006.

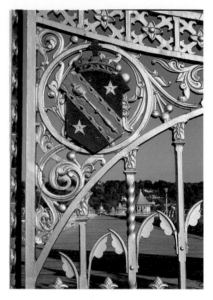

Above: After its closure in 1971, Bangor Garth Pier was saved from demolition by Bangor City Council, which bought the pier for one penny in 1975. Raising funds for its renovation then took a further seven years, and restoration work costing £3.5 million was carried out during 1982–8.

Left: Aerial view of Southport Pier.

However, the demolition of Morecambe Central (1992), Ventnor (1992–3) and Shanklin (1993) reduced the total number of British pleasure piers to just fifty-five at the start of the twenty-first century. Although the Heritage Lottery Fund (HLF) initially supported full restoration of Brighton West Pier, Britain's only other Grade I listed pier, a series of storms and fires during 2003 led to the withdrawal of support by English Heritage and the HLF in 2004. The pier's derelict remnants still remain, and the Brighton West Pier Trust hope to rebuild the pier in some form after 2008.

Preservation and restoration of these enjoyable structures, which blur the distinction between engineering and architecture, continue into the twenty-first century. Their apparently timeless appeal has ensured that most of the remaining piers are supported by pier-preservation trusts or individual pier owners who continue to take on these difficult but rewarding structures. Saltburn Pier was restored in 2000–1, with support from Redcar and Cleveland Borough Council, the Heritage Lottery Fund and the European

The new Southport Pier Pavilion, designed by Liverpool-based architects Shed KM, was opened in 2002. The delicate steel, glass and aluminium pavilion, with its swooping roof, stands on a concrete slab supported by two rows of piles. To the left of the pavilion is the pier's road train; it provides transport along the pier and was augmented by an electrically-driven 100-seater custom built tram in 2005. The Pier stretches across the Marine Lake just south of the Marine Way Bridge, a dramatic floodlit structure that opened in 2004.

Regional Development Fund as well as the Friends of Saltburn Pier. In Suffolk, the stubby 150 foot remnant of Southwold Pier, bought by Chris and Helen Iredale in 1987, has benefited from an almost complete reconstruction, taking its length to 620 feet and including a series of pavilions. New Southwold Pier, which may be regarded as the first new pier of the century, was opened by the Duke of Gloucester on 3 July 2001 in front of a crowd of around 8,000. The pier was bought by Stephen Bournes in 2005, and survived the 9 November 2007 surge tide relatively unscathed.

The HLF supported the restoration of Grade II listed Hastings Pier in 2002, but in 2006 Hastings Borough Council found the structure to be unsafe and it was closed, apart from the entrance buildings. The pier's owners disputed this claim but lost their court case in November 2007. The Council has estimated that the total cost of repairs and maintenance over the next ten years would be around £17.5 million (as opposed to around £4 million for demolition), and in 2008 was consulting with the pier's owners and English Heritage on the best way forward.

Above: Clevedon Pier suffered a partial collapse in 1970, during load testing, cutting off the 1894 pavilion and shelters from the landward end. A lengthy period of fund raising and restoration work followed, including its near-total dismantling, eventually allowing the pier to reopen in 1989; it was 1995 before the pierhead structures were brought back into use. In January 2001 the pier's listed building status was raised from II* to I, and it is now the only accessible and structurally intact Grade I listed pier in Britain.

Saltburn Pier opened in 1869, when its length was 1,500 feet; a long history of storm damage and other problems including a ship collision (1924) ended with restoration during the 1970s and reopening in 1978 at a length of a mere 681 feet. The pier is now the last remaining pleasure pier on the Yorkshire coast, and further restoration of the deck took place in 2000–1.

The Hastings Pier frontage was rebuilt between the First and Second World Wars using ceramic marble, a material produced by Carters of Poole that was highly resistant to seawater. The pier entrance, which was altered again during the 1960s, is opposite the White Rock Pavilion, a theatre built in 1927 and decorated with colourful pictorial relief roundels in Doulton's Polychrome Stoneware designed by the sculptor Gilbert Bayes.

Brighton West Pier in 2001, with only the tiniest of connecting bridges between pavilions and shore. The pier, which has been under threat of demolition since the 1970s, was purchased by the Brighton West Pier Trust in 1984. Storm damage in the late 1980s cut the link between pavilions and shore, but following a grant from the Heritage Lottery Fund in 1996 a steel walkway was built to cross the gap. Following storms and fires in 2003, the pier is now derelict.

Brighton Palace Pier was built in 1891–9 at a cost of £137,000; its length was 1,760 feet. A 1,500-seat theatre opened at the seaward end in 1901 and a pavilion was added to the central section in 1910; the theatre was dismantled in 1986. The pier's delicate ironwork was part of the original oriental-style design by R. St George Moore, who was also responsible for the pier at St Leonards, built in 1888–91 and demolished in 1951.

The Noble Organisation acquired Brighton Palace Pier (now known as Brighton Pier) in 1984 from the Brighton Marine Palace and Pier Company, its original owners. This popular pier is now home to a range of entertainment facilities including a funfair with a helter-skelter, something of a landmark, near the end of the pier.

Construction of New Southwold Pier and its pavilions taking place during 2000. A T-section pierhead is also to be built, enabling passenger vessels to call at the pier, as the 'Belle' steamers did before the original pierhead was destroyed by storms in 1934. The pier, which reopened in 2001, now offers visitors a pier history exhibition, shop, pub and diner as well as an amusement arcade.

Coastal steamer traffic declined between the First and Second World Wars, but its architectural legacy includes Wemyss Bay station, where day-tripping Glaswegians left the train to catch the Rothesay ferry; the adjacent pierhead is reached via a curving, covered wooden walkway. The station, which was rebuilt by the Caledonian Railway in 1903, was designed by the architect James Miller and the engineer Donald Mathieson, who both worked on the extension of Glasgow Central Station (1899–1905).

Although the outlook for several piers is brighter than for many years, in 2007 the National Piers Society was still able to pinpoint the ten piers it felt to be most seriously at risk from demolition or partial collapse, seven of which were wholly or partly closed to the public on safety grounds. The ten were Weston-super-Mare Birnbeck, Hastings, Colwyn Bay Victoria, Ramsey Queen's, Herne Bay, Lowestoft Claremont, Felixstowe, Bognor Regis, Swanage and Totland Bay. In the case of Birnbeck, the regeneration and property company Urban Splash ran an architectural ideas competition in 2007 with the aim of realising the potential of the pier and its site; the winners, Levitate Architecture and Design Studio, were announced in 2008. This combination of exciting new development with historic pier sites may turn out to be the way forward for Britain's piers in the twenty-first century.

Herne Bay Pier reopened after the Second World War but suffered storm damage in 1953 and closed (apart from its shoreward end) in 1968 when it was found to be in a dangerous state. Most of the long, narrow neck of the pier was destroyed by storms on 11 January 1978, leaving this little pier head pavilion, on the former landing stage, isolated in the sea. However, the Herne Bay Pier Trust was set up in 2008 with the aim of raising funds to rebuild the pier.

THE PEOPLE'S PLEASURE PALACES

Such was the popularity of the seaside holiday in the late nineteenth and early twentieth centuries that huge entertainment complexes became necessary to cater for the crowds. These massive leisure facilities, of which Blackpool Tower is the best known, were funded by an array of financial backers, from large industrial concerns to a multitude of small investors, and were largely located within reach of the cities of north-west England. English visitors and sometimes English finance helped the entertainment business flourish in Wales and the Isle of Man, but the English holiday-making masses never reached Scotland. There, resort development was also restricted by climate, and only a few resorts, of which Rothesay was the most significant, could support entertainment buildings approaching the English ones in scale.

The idea of these pleasure palaces originated with the smaller and earlier winter gardens and assembly rooms. The success of the Crystal Palace, initially at the Great Exhibition of 1851 and then at its Sydenham site from 1854, inspired the construction of many smaller iron-and-glass winter gardens at the resorts. However, it was the series of orchestral concerts held at the Crystal Palace, drawing audiences as large as 80,000, that made fashionable the combination of music and large-scale winter garden. Three massive seaside winter gardens were built: at Southport in 1874, where the Manchester architects Maxwell & Tuke built what was advertised as 'the largest conservatory in England'; at Bournemouth (1875–6); and at Torquay (1878–81). The last is the only survivor, having been sold to Great Yarmouth Council in 1903, dismantled, shipped round the coast and re-erected at the town's Wellington Pier; the Southport and Bournemouth winter gardens were demolished during the 1930s. Along with the Crystal Palace, Torquay's winter garden is one of the few theoretically demountable buildings actually to be moved and rebuilt.

Another international exhibition, the 1889 Paris Exposition Universelle, provided the next stimulus for seaside building. Its iconic Eiffel Tower, then the tallest building in the world at 984 feet, was visited by nearly two million

Opposite: The theatre at the Queen's Palace, Rhyl, which was designed by C. J. Richardson and built in 1902. The theatre alone was rebuilt after the 1907 fire, without the domed pavilion, and is still extant, although its auditorium was reconstructed in 1928.

Tynemouth Winter Garden was built above the resort's Long Sands in 1876–8, its designers being the London partnership of John Norton, architect to the Crystal Palace Company estate, and Philip Masey. The spectacular structure included a basement aquarium and a winter garden over 200 feet long. The building was never a financial success, and, despite being Britain's sole remaining brick-façaded winter garden, was not a listed building. It burned down on 10 February 1996.

people during the exhibition and rapidly recouped its cost. The idea of a tower as a profitable attraction quickly took root at the British seaside, where the tower could be seen as a vertical version of the pier, combining a view with other entertainments. Patents for towers in a wide variety of shapes, heights and construction systems were granted, although most of these were never built. The first attempt, at Wembley (where the tower was intended to be the centre of a vast outdoor amusement park), reached the height of 155 feet before funding ran out; this failure appeared to deter potential investors in seaside towers.

A tower for Blackpool was originally proposed by the Standard Contract and Debenture Corporation, a property company with Isle of Man and London connections, although the more locally based Blackpool Tower Company took over the site in 1891. A design competition for the tower was won by Maxwell & Tuke and construction began in mid 1891; R. J. G. Read of Westminster was the consulting engineer. The 500-foot tower itself was built by the end of 1893 but the complex of buildings below was only finished after the Tower opened to the public on Whit Monday 1894. Early customers eventually experienced an accumulation of delights previously unknown at any single British entertainment venue: an aquarium and menagerie, a circus cunningly fitted into the area between the four legs of the tower, the lift ride to the top of the tower, the Grand Pavilion (later the Tower Ballroom) and a range of shops, bars and cafés, all in a building that was imposing without and highly decorative within. Colourful high-relief Burmantofts ceramic panels brightened the corridors while the circus was tricked out with glittering, Moorish-style ceramic ornament.

The Tower was an undoubted success, much to the consternation of other Blackpool entertainment promoters, especially those of the nearby Winter Gardens.

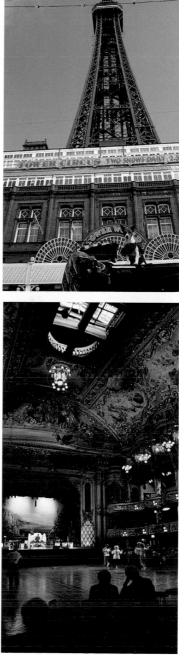

Above: The tiered structure of Torquay (later Great Yarmouth) Winter Gardens was more like that of a horticultural winter garden than the great seaside conservatories at Southport and Bournemouth. The Torquay glasshouse had no curved panes and little decoration apart from floral motifs on the ironwork. It was 170 feet long and measured 83 feet to the top of the lantern.

Top right: The exterior of Blackpool Tower Buildings, overlooking the promenade, was far from decorative, its combination of red brick and elaborate terracotta dressings making the structure appear more like a department store than an entertainment centre. Its original design did indeed include two shopping arcades, although these were never built.

Bottom right: Blackpool Tower's Grand Pavilion was converted to the Tower Ballroom by Frank Matcham in 1898–9. The style was French Renaissance and the effect overwhelming; the ballroom, said to be one of the three finest in Britain, was an instant success. Matcham's important interior was burnt out during 1956 but was reinstated to exactly the original design, reopening in 1958.

Below: Blackpool Winter Gardens was given a dramatic new appearance from 1929, when its façade was clad in sparkling white faience supplied by Shaws of Darwen. The order, which included blue and yellow decorative elements such as the lettering emphasising the archway, was worth £22,638 to the firm.

Left: In contrast to its forbidding exterior, Blackpool Tower's interior is highly decorative. This low-relief Burmantofts faience panel with rich turquoise glaze is one of a series lining the main staircase; the designer was E. Caldwell Spruce, a principal modeller at the Leeds firm. Other panels show fishes, cherubs and children.

Right: New Brighton Tower, completed in 1898, was an octagonal complex of buildings in red Ruabon brick with terracotta and stone dressings; the octagonal tower rose from its centre. The unsuccessful tower met the same fate as the town's pier, which was closed in 1972 and demolished in 1977.

The Winter Gardens began life in 1878 as an elegant, apsidal-ended theatre with a glass-roofed promenade running around its base. To this was added in 1889 an opera house by the leading theatre designer Frank Matcham, and then, stung by competition from the Tower, the ornate Empress Ballroom (by the architects Mangnall & Littlewoods) in 1896. The Tower and Winter Gardens continued trying to outdo each other until the turn of the century; they were joined by a third pleasure palace, only a few streets away, when the Alhambra opened in 1899. This massive building, designed by the architects Wylson & Long, contained three huge performance spaces: a 2,000-seat circus, a ballroom for 3,000 dancers and a 3,000-seat theatre. Even for Blackpool this was a palace too far and the receivers were brought in during 1902. The Blackpool Tower Company purchased the Alhambra in the following year, called in Frank Matcham to redesign its interior and opened it in 1904 as the Palace. In 1914 an underground passage was created joining Tower and Palace so that pleasure-seekers could avoid the promenade gales; however, the Palace was demolished in 1961.

At New Brighton, Wirral, another and taller tower was under construction in 1897, again designed by Maxwell & Tuke. The New Brighton Tower and Recreation Company initially found capital easy to come by as a result of Blackpool Tower's success and went for an altogether grander complex: the

Morecambe Tower, which stood at the north-eastern end of the town's seafront from 1899, was bought by the Morecambe Tower and Estates Company in 1909 after its original owners had run into financial problems. More of the tower's base buildings were then completed, including the pavilion (1909) and a ballroom (1911), and the enterprise was marketed as a fairground (an early theme park), but with little success. The tower itself did not survive the 1914–18 war, but it was 1961 before the remaining base buildings were demolished.

eight legs of the 576-foot high tower enclosed the 3,000-seat Grand Tower Theatre, the largest theatre in the country outside London; there was also a ballroom with capacity for 2,000, a winter garden and other entertainments. The landmark building opened in 1898 but could never draw the enormous number of visitors necessary for profitability; the tower itself was demolished

The architects of Southend Kursaal, seen here in 2001, were George Sherrin and John Clarke of London. The much-altered interior originally included a circus and a theatre, actually a flat-floored music hall that could double as a ballroom. The Burton brewing company Samuel Allsopp's had taken over the building by 1903, and later developments concentrated on the amusement park rather than the Kursaal itself.

The Queen's Palace at Rhyl, seen here around 1905. It was lost to fire in 1907, although another domed entertainment centre, the Rhyl Pavilion, was erected near the seafront in 1908. Rhyl Pier, built by James Brunlees in 1867, was demolished in 1973.

in 1919–21 and the remaining buildings burned out in 1969. Even shorter-lived was Morecambe's attempt at a tower-cum-pleasure palace, the skeleton of which was built in 1899–1900. The Morecambe Tower, with all its base buildings and pleasure grounds, was intended to provide a wholly oriental environment, including a bazaar and ethnic stallholders, its visitors being carried to the top of the cone-shaped tower by a spiral tramway. The venture did not prosper and the tower itself was dismantled during the First World War.

Away from the north-west, Southend Kursaal (whose guidebook compared its attractions to Blackpool's Winter Gardens) was rather more successful, its

The white dome of Spanish City (1911) originally marked the presence on Whitley Bay seafront of a leisure complex including a large flat-floored theatre. This unusual pleasure dome, 50 feet in diameter, was constructed using the Hennebique reinforced concrete system (first used in Britain in 1897); even in the 1970s the Spanish City dome was still thought to be second in size only to that of St Paul's Cathedral. The architects were the Newcastle upon Tyne practice of James Thoburn Cackett and Robert Burns Dick.

1898 building being topped by a dome and including a range of attractions as well as ninety shops; the building, although much altered, still stands. The last of the pleasure domes, the Queen's Palace, was built at Rhyl in 1902 to cater mainly for Lancashire trippers. Under its great glazed dome was a ballroom with sprung parquet floor on which 2,000 couples could dance, a theatre, a winter garden, forty shops, a zoo, a waxworks, a native village and – beneath the ballroom – an imitation Venice with real canals. The Queen's Palace was destroyed by fire in 1907, leaving only Blackpool's Tower and Winter Gardens and the much-changed Southend Kursaal to remind us of this era of mass entertainment and massive buildings.

Even as some of the largest indoor entertainment complexes were still being built, outdoor entertainment on a similar scale, in the form of the amusement park, was becoming popular. At Blackpool the beginnings of a fairground appeared on the South Shore in the early 1890s, with larger rides being introduced from 1904. The fairground, which was known as the Pleasure Beach from 1906, had become the biggest and most modern amusement park in Britain by 1909; its owners formed the private company Blackpool Pleasure Beach Limited in 1910. Along with the largest of the seaside piers and their varied facilities, the amusement parks at Blackpool and elsewhere became outdoor pleasure palaces, all-purpose leisure environments that were the forerunners of modern theme parks.

The first British example of a Warwick's Revolving Tower (left) was built on Great Yarmouth seafront, just north of Britannia Pier, in 1897; the first ever had been put up in Atlantic City, New Jersey. The Yarmouth tower continued in operation until 1939, although the revolving mechanism had ceased to function after the First World War; it was demolished in 1941.

ENTERTAINMENT ASHORE

WHEN seaside resorts were simply watering places, leisure at the seaside was an elegant affair of quiet enjoyment, simple contemplation of the view from a promenade shelter, but with the crowds came the need for novelty attractions that were also profitable. The view from the promenade was free but could be commercialised by means of enticing the customer to pay for its enhancement. A series of observation towers known as Warwick's Revolving Towers was built by the London engineer Thomas Warwick at Great Yarmouth, Cleethorpes, Morecambe, Douglas, Scarborough and Southend during 1897–1902. These inelegant latticework structures, about 150 feet high, were hexagonal in cross-section and carried a platform on which a carriage revolved. Thus up to 200 passengers at a time were simultaneously lifted and rotated to enjoy a panoramic view; the power was provided by a steam engine that generated electricity. Cliff railways also offered the combination of view and transportation. The first seaside cliff railway was built at Scarborough's South Cliff in 1875 and others followed, for instance at Saltburn (1884) and Hastings East Cliff (1903); the station buildings, their design reminiscent of small toll-houses, often form an attractive part of the townscape.

The view could also be transformed by the use of electric lighting. Blackpool Illuminations began life in 1897 when the first illuminated trams trundled along the promenade to mark Queen Victoria's Diamond Jubilee. The combination of coloured lights and movement was instantly successful, and the concept was expanded from 1912 to include strings of electric lights hung from lamp-posts and across arches. Blackpool Casino, built at the entrance to the Pleasure Beach in 1913, was one of several contemporary seaside buildings to be defined by their lavish use of electric lighting. This 700-seat cinema was constructed from reinforced concrete in the style of an Indian palace; at night, the fantastic domed Casino glittered at the end of the promenade, drawing holiday-makers toward the Pleasure Beach. Great Yarmouth's Gem Cinema, built in 1908 by the local architect Arthur S. Hewitt, was known as 'The Palace of 5,000 Lights', although this effect was

Opposite: Earl De La Warr, a socialist, was Mayor of Bexhill during 1932–4 and the little town's major landowner. In 1933 he organised an architectural competition for a Modernist public building, attracting 230 entries, and put up £100,000 to see construction of the welded steel-framed De La Warr Pavilion completed in 1936. Controversy over its design and philosophy brought his period as Mayor to an end.

Saltburn's inclined tramway (foreground) opened in 1884. It was Britain's third cliff lift, the first two having been built at Scarborough in 1875 and 1881. The water-balanced tramway replaced a vertical hoist that had carried passengers between cliff and beach during 1870–83; the hoist was designed by John Anderson, who was also engineer for Saltburn Pier.

Blackpool Illuminations in 1996. The Tower has featured in the Illuminations since 1925, when its lighting carried the message 'Wonderland of the World'. More than 10,000 bulbs are required to light the tower.

The Casino, a cinema, was built at Blackpool Pleasure Beach in 1913. From 1910 the Pleasure Beach began to provide indoor entertainments, the first being the Naval Spectatorium, a massive circular building in which American Civil War naval battles were replayed using lighting and mechanical devices.

actually achieved by fixing 1,500 electric light bulbs to its ornate buff terracotta façade. There were also several water parks whose exotic structures were illuminated by night, as at Scarborough's Northstead Manor Gardens or Great Yarmouth's Waterways, where the boats were decorated fairground-style and daytime colour was provided by mass flower-bedding. Colour, lights and water also came together at the circus, where the grand finale at technically sophisticated venues like Great Yarmouth's Hippodrome, built in 1903, was the water spectacle, initially performed in Rome's Colosseum; at the Blackpool Tower circus it took only two minutes for 40,000 gallons of water to flood the ring and transform the arena.

Up to the mid 1920s, traditional seaside design changed little, retaining its emphasis on prefabrication and cosy vernacular but sometimes idiosyncratic structures. Winter gardens in various formats remained popular: Walter MacFarlane's Saracen Foundry in Glasgow supplied prefabricated components for the not dissimilar pair Ryde Pavilion (1923–6) and the domed Rothesay Winter Gardens (1923–4), both of which still survive, but the seaside was soon to become the most receptive location in Britain for architecture of the Modern Movement.

The first significant Modernist structure to appear at the seaside was the Royal Corinthian Yacht Club, designed by the architect Joseph Emberton and built at Burnham-on-Crouch in 1931. Its long, low, clean white lines and extravagant horizontal glazing brought to mind sunshine, elegance and a streamlined brand of leisure rather different from that associated with Victorian decorative excesses. Other fine examples of international Modernism followed, including the Midland Hotel, Morecambe (1932–3), by the architect Oliver Hill, built for the London Midland & Scottish Railway

Above left: Great Yarmouth's Gem (later Windmill) Cinema, which opened in 1908, was probably England's first purpose-built seaside cinema, although the flat-floored hall could also be used for variety performances.

Above right: Great Yarmouth's Empire Cinema opened in July 1911; it was built for the Yarmouth and Gorleston Investment and Building Company and was designed by the architect Arthur S. Hewitt, who was also responsible for the nearby Gem Cinema. Its Edwardian baroque façade, a triumphal arch framed by giant, fluted Ionic columns, was clad in Burmantofts vitreous terracotta. The interior was in sumptuous Louis XIV style.

41

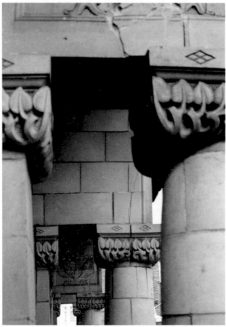

Above left:
Great Yarmouth Hippodrome, an unusual purpose-built circus seating 2,500, was designed by the architect Ralph Scott Cockrill (1879–1956) and opened in 1903. Three stained-glass windows depicting chariot racing originally graced the entrance façade.

Above:
The manufacturer of Great Yarmouth Hippodrome's delicate Art Nouveau terracotta is unknown, but may perhaps be Doulton of Lambeth. The circus had a double-roof structure and 2-foot-thick concrete walls to provide adequate noise insulation.

Left:
The architect of Great Yarmouth Hippodrome, Ralph Scott Cockrill, had at least two younger brothers who became architects, while his architect father – the borough surveyor J. W. Cockrill – was also the inventor of the Cockrill wall facing tile patented with Doulton of Lambeth in 1893. Ralph Scott Cockrill's grandfather was William Cockrill, a builder and developer from nearby Gorleston-on-Sea.

At the centre of Torquay's seafront is the Pavilion (1911–12). Its original 1896 design was by Edward Rogers, but construction was completed after his death by Torbay's borough engineer Henry Augustus Garrett. The steel-framed building is clad in white Doulton Carraraware with pale-green banded decoration. The Pavilion was saved from the threat of demolition in the early 1970s and remodelled in 1986–7 as a shopping arcade; its 1939 extension was removed, and the eastern façade reconstructed in specially manufactured faience blocks.

and a descendant of many great resort hotels, the grandest of which was Scarborough's Grand Hotel (1863–7). The Midland was rather Art Deco in feel and featured artworks by Eric Gill and Eric Ravilious as well as rugs by Marion Dorn. Restoration of the Midland Hotel began in 2005 and was completed in June 2008, when the hotel reopened. The much-photographed De La Warr Pavilion, Bexhill (1933–6), was designed by architects Erich Mendelsohn and Serge Chermayeff and offered the somewhat surprised residents of the little seaside town a repertory theatre, tea dances,

Rothesay Winter Gardens originated around 1895 as an octagonal bandstand on the Esplanade. In 1923–4 a circular domed structure, prefabricated at Walter MacFarlane's Saracen Foundry, was added to cover the seating area, while the bandstand was also roofed over and an entrance was created between twin pagoda-style square towers. The building is now the Isle of Bute Discovery Centre.

The domed interior of Rothesay Winter Gardens, showing some of the sixteen steel radial supporting ribs that centre on a pendulous faience light fitting. There is much Art Nouveau cast-iron ornament on the building's exterior (where a walkway circles the dome), and even the iron ventilation grilles are highly decorative.

a restaurant and a reading room. Afternoon tea may still be taken on its serene sunlit balconies, which look all the better since the building's £8 million restoration, by architect John McAslan and Partners, was finished in 2005.

Less well known examples of seaside Modernism include Ventnor Winter Gardens (1935), Rothesay Pavilion (1938) and even the now demolished Derby Baths (1938–9) in Blackpool, a daring yellow and lime-green ceramic box whose walls were cut through by porthole windows and decorated with fishy roundels; the faience was by Shaws of Darwen while the design was by

The Royal Corinthian Yacht Club, built at Burnham-on-Crouch in 1931. The steel-framed structure stands on a concrete platform supported by stilts in the water, its long horizontal windows providing commanding views across the estuary. It was a dramatic and initially controversial replacement for the Yacht Club's previous premises, a small weather-boarded clubhouse.

The broad half-drum of the café at Rothesay Pavilion (1938) appears to have taken at least some inspiration from Bexhill's Pavilion; the Rothesay design was a competition-winning entry from the architect James Carrick. Inside is a rectangular auditorium and a grand Art Deco staircase. Although the stylish building is still very much in use, the ground level glazing has been (temporarily) defaced by advertisements.

Blackpool Casino, built at the Pleasure Beach in 1939, rests on a base of reinforced concrete above the sandy subsoil. The Trussed Concrete and Steel Company (Truscon) designed the Casino's reinforced-concrete structure; the thin pre-cast concrete facing panels were made in Holland, then delivered to Blackpool by barge. Inside the Casino was a series of restaurants, everything from First Class to Soda Fountain, while its banqueting room could seat 1,000 people.

The Jubilee Pool, Penzance (1935), is superbly situated on a promontory, with views towards St Michael's Mount and Newlyn. The tidal pool was designed by the borough engineer F. Latham and incorporated stepped terraces for sunbathing as well as floodlights to allow for swimming after sunset.

Top left: Paignton Festival Hall, built on the town's Esplanade in 1962 and designed by the architect C. F. J. Thurley. Just to the north is Paignton Pier, built in 1878–9 to the design of local architect George Soudon Bridgman (1839–1925), which became a regular port of call for pleasure steamers crossing Torbay; it was reopened in 1995 after restoration work.

Bottom left: Torquay's Princess Theatre at dusk, seen from Princess Pier. The theatre, in style a Scandinavian variation on the Festival Hall theme, was built in the 1960s, along with the pier's central shelter (1965), its angled glazing being a typical 1960s affectation. The pier itself dates from 1890, although most of its later steel substructure was replaced during 1978–9 as it had become corroded.

Above: Saltdean Lido (1938), designed by R. W. H. Jones, was the first British lido to become a listed building. Its central two-storey pavilion contained a café and sunbathing terraces, while changing rooms occupied the wings; a diving board originally stood opposite the café. A tunnel beneath the coast road links the lido to the beach.

the borough surveyor, John C. Robinson. Also in Blackpool, the Pleasure Beach Casino was demolished in 1937 to be succeeded in 1939 by Joseph Emberton's circular white Casino, its dizzy spiral stair tower suggestive of delights within the amusement park. Emberton worked at the Pleasure Beach from 1933, building many rides for the owners, who wished for a 'unified modern design'; fun and Modernism were securely joined in the public mind. Perhaps the purest expression of seaside modern style were the lidos, in particular the languid curves of the Jubilee Pool in Penzance (1935), Saltdean Lido (1938) and the massive New Brighton Lido (1934), said to have the largest outdoor pool in Europe but demolished in 1990.

Lowestoft's East Point Pavilion (1997), a café and information centre, with the Royal Norfolk and Suffolk Yacht Club (1902–3) in the background. The Norwich architect George Skipper produced an L-shaped plan to utilise the Yacht Club's difficult triangular site; the building is topped by a fully glazed observation room under a copper dome.

A trickle of good seaside buildings continued to be constructed into the 1950s and early 1960s, for instance Dunoon Queen's Hall (1955–8) by the Glasgow architect Ninian Johnston, who used a jolly variety of materials in this Festival-of-Britain inspired replacement for an Edwardian pavilion opposite the pier, and Paignton's Festival Hall (1962), a colourful presence on the promenade. However, the decline in seaside holiday-making after the 1960s produced an increase in buildings designed to attract a new type of visitor to the resorts. Sadly, the results – including several conference centres and leisure centres, as at Cleethorpes, where the Leisure Centre (1983)

The Landmark Theatre was built on Ilfracombe's seafront in 1997 to replace the Victoria Pavilion Theatre (1925), which had been damaged by a storm in 1990. The designers of the striking conical structures, their forms based on traditional glass-making kilns or cones, were Tim Ronalds Architects. Over 300,000 bricks, made from German clay fired in Belgium, were laid during construction of the Landmark, which provides two main performance spaces, one of them flat-floored.

Left: This fishy artwork above the flood barrier on Southport's Marine Drive formed part of the 1998 programme of improvements to the town's sea defences, along with a pair of monstrous fish sculpted in the concrete of the sea wall adjacent to the pier.

Right: Looking south along the South Promenade Improvement Scheme at Bridlington, a creative collaboration between the artist Bruce McLean and the architects Bauman Lyons. The design included buildings (a café-bar, chalets, toilets, office, deckchair store), landscaping (built-in terrazzo street furniture, a paddling pool) and public art knitted together by the 'Nautical Mile', a mile-long terrazzo pavement sculpture with inset text by Mel Gooding.

dominates the southern end of the beach – were often nondescript, bulky and architecturally undistinguished.

Latterly, new thinking about the changed role of the resorts has brought high-quality architecture back to the seaside, where it belongs. During the 1990s the Tate St Ives (1993) led a renewal of interest in the Cornish resort and its artists, while Lowestoft's East Point Pavilion (an updated winter garden opened in 1997) at last went some way to capitalising on the resort's easterly location. More exciting is the National Trust's hi-tech White Cliffs Centre (2000), Dover, which brilliantly exploits the ever-changing view of shipping below, and Ilfracombe's Landmark Theatre (1997), where the nautical style of the 1950s has been surprisingly reinvented and renewed. Artworks have been integrated into promenade developments at Southport (partly driven by the need to improve sea defences) and in the South Promenade Improvement Scheme at Bridlington, which opened in 1998 and won a RIBA award. Here, collaboration between artists and architects resulted in a promenade environment so successful that visitor numbers increased by 20 per cent.

The twenty-first century has already seen increased interest in the seaside by bodies such as English Heritage, the Victorian Society and CABE (the Commission for Architecture and the Built Environment) as well as a number of spectacular new seaside buildings. In 2003 a delicate, white gull-wing-shaped bandstand, the work of Niall McLaughlin Architects, appeared in front of Bexhill's De La Warr Pavilion. The same firm was also responsible for the timber-frame and glass design of the new café at Deal Pier, under construction in 2007–8. Blackpool's South Shore Promenade now sports a series of hi-tech swivelling wind shelters (2006, architect Ian McChesney), a new take on the Victorian seaside shelter, while a design competition organised by artist Michael Trainor resulted in a series of radically different beach huts being installed at Mablethorpe in 2007, with more promised for 2008. One of the most welcome new seaside structures was the East Beach Café (2007) at Littlehampton, an intriguing

One of a series of swivelling wind shelters on Blackpool's South Shore Promenade that were installed in 2006 as part of the Great Promenade Show of public artworks. The stainless steel shelter is 26 feet tall, rotates on a turntable 13 feet in diameter, and was designed by the architect Ian McChesney in collaboration with engineers Atelier One. Each shelter seats up to eight people and turns to keep its occupants away from the prevailing wind. The structure's form is similar to an aircraft wing, and vibrates in strong gusts of wind.

design by Thomas Heatherwick in what appears to be crumpled, rusting iron. Perhaps the most unusual of the new century's installations was the sculpture 'Couple' by Sean Henry, a pair of 16-foot-tall bronze figures positioned out on the breakwater at Newbiggin by the Sea in Northumberland, commissioned as part of the town's beach regeneration project.

Future projects include the Turner Contemporary at Margate, an international art gallery with a dramatic setting overlooking the bay; designed by David Chipperfield Architects, it is scheduled to open in 2010. Construction of the Brighton Tower, an observation tower based at the landward end of the West Pier, was due to begin in 2008. Designed by Marks Barfield, architects of the London Eye, the 600-foot-high tower will allow passengers to rise 456 feet up the tower in a viewing pod. Once construction work on the Tower is in progress, the Brighton West Pier Trust hopes to begin planning the recreation of the sea-based pier. It seems that the seaside is once again fashionable in the twenty-first century.

The iconic East Beach Café at Littlehampton officially opened on 19 June 2007. The design, by the Heatherwick Studio, resembles a huge piece of driftwood washed up on the beach; the rippling mild steel shell forms the building's structure and will rust as it ages. The complex construction also used the expertise of local steelworks Littlehampton Welding and London-based engineering consultants Adams Kara Taylor.

LIVING AND WORKING AT THE SEASIDE

FAR from being a mundane backdrop for exotic entertainment architecture, some seaside homes – from the delightfully Gothick *cottages ornés* of Regency Sidmouth to holiday villages such as Thorpeness or Portmeirion – are equally inventive. Although the flat-roofed Modern Movement house found a welcome home at the seaside in the 1930s, there was still opportunity for new interpretations of traditional seaside colour, as at San Remo Towers, Boscombe (1936–8), a huge block of flats embellished with candy-striped faience. Although beach huts are little more than wooden huts with railed front verandas, having originated with the bathing machines of the Regency seaside, they can be endlessly decorative and have always been popular, despite occasionally being seen as deeply unfashionable. By the late 1990s they were in short supply in some resorts, and new 'huts' were built at Lowestoft, Brighton (actually floating flats at Brighton Marina) and Bridlington, where high-quality chalets were included in the South Promenade Improvement Scheme.

The architecture of the working seaside, like the red-and-white-striped Gribbin seamark near Fowey and the black net lofts of Hastings, gave rise to 1950s definitions of the nautical style: strong, geometric form combined with solid, bright colour. Now, everyday structures including lifeboat stations and beach cafés contribute to good seaside design, while even such an unlikely candidate as Southern Water's waste-water treatment works at Ventnor (2000), topped by an open circular viewing platform, has made a landmark out of a potential eyesore. From beach huts and Blackpool Tower to piers and promenades, a distinctively British style of seaside architecture has evolved, rooted in inventiveness and idiosyncrasy. It encompasses dynamic Victorian orientalism and cool 1930s modernism as well as today's hi-tech, artistically inspired structures and appears to be full of promise for the twenty-first-century seaside.

Opposite: The traditional beach amusement of the donkey ride is still available at Blackpool – although not on Fridays, when a local by-law gives the animals a day off; in the background is the North Pier. Camels were once tried as donkey substitutes, but Blackpool's wet summers were not to their liking.

The Egyptian House in Penzance was built around 1835 as a museum and geological repository. It is a rare surviving example of the style popular after Napoleon's 1798 campaign in Egypt; its Coade-stone ornamentation includes Egyptian figures and winged serpents. The house is now owned by the Landmark Trust.

A la Ronde, near Exmouth, is a unique sixteen-sided *cottage orné* built in 1798 for Jane Parminter, daughter of a Devon merchant, and her cousin Mary Parminter on their return from a ten-year European Grand Tour; the site has superb views over Exmouth and the Exe estuary. The house, which was bought by the National Trust in 1991, is crowned by the Shell Gallery, an elaborate featherwork and shell fantasy room created over many years by the Parminters.

Traditional seaside images on a roadside tile panel made by Carter's of Poole in the 1950s and designed by Arthur Nickols. These tubelined panels, showing yachts in Poole Harbour, once graced local approach roads and the Poole promenade. They were also made for other towns including Swanage and Sandbanks, where one is still extant in its original position near the harbour mouth.

Left top: A modern take on traditional beach-hut design at Lowestoft, where these colourful huts were built near the Claremont Pier, above the town's South Beach, during the late 1990s.

Left middle: Chalets on Princess Mary Promenade, Bridlington, built in 1998 as part of the South Promenade Improvement Scheme. Each of the thirty-seven chalets has individual access to the promenade and thence the beach by a 3-foot-wide wooden bridge across the water channel.

Left bottom: Workaday beach huts at Southwold; the lifeguards' (right) and fishermen's huts, with their strong colours and forms, display a stark contrast to the often humorous decoration shown by the typical holiday-maker's beach hut.

Below: The dazzling Gribbin daymark on Gribbin Head, near Fowey in Cornwall, was erected in 1832 to enable sailors to distinguish between Gribbin Head and the similarly shaped St Anthony's Head to the west at the entrance to Falmouth Bay. The Gribbin is 80 feet in height.

Peters Tower (right) was built at Lympstone, on the Exe estuary, in 1855 by William Peters as a memorial to his wife Mary Jane. The family, who lived nearby, gave the tower to the Landmark Trust in 1979. The tower, which carries a clock, was originally used as a refuge for fishermen; after restoration, and installation of a spectacular spiral staircase, the tower is now in use as a holiday home.

The Boston Deep Sea Fisheries office, opposite Lowestoft's harbour, was built by Consolidated Fisheries and known as Columbus Buildings. The white faience-façaded block has twin tiled panels of galleons – presumably representations of the Niña, the Pinta and the Santa Maria – at first-floor level; these brightly coloured, beautifully designed panels were probably manufactured by Doulton of Lambeth.

Southern Water's waste-water treatment works at Eastbourne could be a modern brown-brick interpretation of a Martello tower. The design of essential facilities such as these is much improved; the earlier Yorkshire Water pumping station on Bridlington's seafront was generally viewed as such an eyesore that it had to be re-clad when the promenade was improved in the 1990s.

Right: The waste-water treatment works built by
Southern Water at Ventnor, on the south coast of
the Isle of Wight, was initially controversial
because of its situation on the resort's beach just
below the 1930s Winter Gardens. Perhaps its
well-designed viewing gallery will eventually take
the place of Ventnor's Royal Victoria Pier,
demolished in 1993, as a promenading venue.

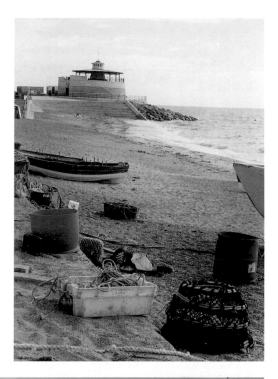

Below: Tinside Lido (1935) protrudes into the
sea below Plymouth Hoe; the architect was J. S.
Wibberley, the borough engineer. With its three
fountains and spectacular views into Plymouth
Sound, the pool was initially popular, but closed in
1992 after attendances declined and repair bills
increased. A £3.4 million refurbishment enabled
the pool, listed Grade II in 1998, to reopen in
2003. Two of the three original fountains were
replicated while the third was replaced by a
33-foot-high water jet.

Saltburn was faced with the possible loss of its pier in 1975, when the local council, owners of the pier since 1938, requested permission to demolish the structure. A public enquiry decided that only the far end of the pier should be removed, and it reopened (after restoration) in 1978; further restoration took place in 2000–1.

Penarth Pier was built in 1894–5, and a wooden pavilion added to its seaward end in 1907; the shore-end pavilion (which still retains its turnstiles) was built in 1927–8. The first pavilion and several shelters were destroyed in a fire on August Bank Holiday 1931. The pier was completely restored during 1994–8.

Mumbles Pier, about 5 miles south-west of Swansea along the Gower peninsula, opened in 1898 as the terminus of the Swansea and Mumbles Railway. It was designed by W. Sutcliffe Marsh using cast iron piles and lattice steelwork, and was originally 835 feet long. The walkway to the lifeboat slipway was added in 1916, with its boathouse (just visible on the left) built in 1922. Following the Second World War, much of the pier was reconstructed before it reopened in 1956. Although the railway line closed in 1960, the pier – which never had an ornate pavilion – continues to attract anglers and tourists.

Right: The landmark Observation Tower (2005) on Southend's Pier Hill provides easy access to the pier entrance by means of a lift. The Adventure Island fun park, with its four roller coasters, surrounds the shore end of the pier, while just to the west is the distinctive blue and yellow Three Shells Café (1982), an essay in concrete.

Below: Pontin's Holiday Village, beside Ainsdale Beach and just south of Southport, opened in 1970, its 700 self-catering chalets being the holiday camp firm's first development in the north of England. Seen from the air, it is particularly notable for its rigid geometric layout. Despite competition from foreign holidays – Pontin's also opened their Hotel Pontinental in Torremolinos in 1970 – the Southport holiday park is still in operation by Pontin's.

Below right: The Column was erected at West Kirby, Cheshire, in 1841 by the Trustees of the Liverpool Docks. It took the place of an old windmill, destroyed by a gale in 1839, which had previously been used by mariners as a navigational aid. The stone-built daymark, largely a Doric column in form, overlooks the Dee estuary; there is an expansive view from its site on Caldy Hill.

FURTHER READING

Adamson, Simon H. *Seaside Piers*. Batsford, 1977.

Bainbridge, Cyril. *Pavilions on the Sea: A History of the Seaside Pleasure Pier*. Robert Hale, 1986.

Barker, Nigel; Brodie, Allan; Dermott, Nick; Jessop, Lucy; and Winter, Gary. *Margate's Seaside Heritage*. English Heritage, 2007.

Boulton & Paul Ltd 1898 Catalogue. Algrove Publishing (Ottawa), 1998.

Braggs, Steven, and Harris, Diane. *Sun, Sea and Sand: The Great British Seaside Holiday*. NPI Media Group, 2006.

Brodie, Allan; Sargent, Andrew; and Winter, Gary. Seaside Holidays in the Past. English Heritage, 2005.

Brodie, Allan, and Winter, Gary. *England's Seaside Resorts*. English Heritage, 2007.

Crowe, Ken. Kursaal Memories: A history of Southend's amusement park. Skelter Publishing, 2003.

Curtis, Bill. *Blackpool Tower*. Terence Dalton, 1988.

Easdown, Martin. *Piers of Kent*. NPI Media Group, 2007.

Easdown, Martin. *Southend Pier*. NPI Media Group, 2007.

Fischer, Richard, and Walton, John. *British Piers*. Thames & Hudson, 1987.

Gray, Fred. *Walking on Water: The West Pier Story*. Brighton West Pier Trust, 1998.

Gray, Fred. *Designing the Seaside: Architecture, Society and Nature*. Reaktion Books, 2006.

Green, Rod. *Beach Huts*. Cassell Illustrated, 2005.

Hix, John. *The Glasshouse*. Phaidon, 1996.

Ind, Rosemary. *Emberton*. Scolar Press, 1983.

Lindley, Kenneth. *Seaside Architecture*. Hugh Evelyn, 1973.

McLean, Bruce; Lyons, Bauman; and Gooding, Mel. *Promenade: An Architectural Collaboration for Bridlington*. East Riding of Yorkshire Council, 2001.

Mason, Timothy. *Shifting Sands: Design and the Changing Image of English Seaside Towns*. English Heritage and CABE, 2003.

Mawson, Chris, and Riding, Richard. *British Seaside Piers*. Ian Allen, 2008.

Mickleburgh, Tim. *Guide to British Piers*. National Piers Society, 1998.

Mickleburgh, Tim. *Glory Days: Piers*. Ian Allan Publishing, 1999.

Pearson, Lynn. *The People's Palaces: Seaside Pleasure Buildings 1870–1914*. Barracuda, 1991.

Pearson, Lynn. *Amusement Machines*. Shire Publications, 1992.

Pearson, Lynn. *Lighthouses*. Shire Publications, 1995.

Pearson, Lynn. 'Tile and Tide: Seaside Ceramics', *TACtile: Newsletter of the Tiles and Architectural Ceramics Society*, 53–58 (2000–2).

Powers, Alan (editor). *Farewell My Lido.* Thirties Society, 1991.

Rutherford, Jessica. *The Royal Pavilion.* Brighton Borough Council, 1995.

Samuelson, Dale. *The American Amusement Park.* MBI Publishing (St Paul, Minnesota), 2001.

Saunders, David. *Britain's Maritime Memorials and Mementoes.* Patrick Stephens, 1996.

Smith, Janet. *Liquid Assets: The lidos and open air swimming pools of Britain.* English Heritage, 2005.

Turner, Keith. *Pier Railways and Tramways of the British Isles.* Oakwood Press, 1999.

Walton, John K. *The English Seaside Resort: A Social History, 1750–1914.* Leicester University Press, 1983.

Walton, John K. *Fish and Chips and the British Working Class, 1870–1940.* Leicester University Press, 1992.

Walton, John K. *The British Seaside: Holidays and Resorts in the Twentieth Century.* Manchester University Press, 2000.

Walton, John K. *Riding on Rainbows: Blackpool Pleasure Beach and its place in British popular culture.* Skelter Publishing, 2007.

Ward, Colin, and Hardy, Dennis. *Goodnight Campers! The History of the British Holiday Camp.* Mansell, 1986.

Williams, Peter. *The English Seaside and its Architecture.* English Heritage, 2005.

Wood, Chris. *Walking Over the Waves: Quintessential British Seaside Piers.* Whittles Publishing, 2008.

Woodhams, John. *Funicular Railways.* Shire Publications, 1989.

The National Piers Society is a registered charity that aims to promote and sustain interest in the preservation and continued enjoyment of seaside piers. The Society can be contacted at Flat 1, 128 Gloucester Terrace, London W2 6HP or see the NPS website: www.piers.co.uk.

PLACES TO VISIT

There are fifty-five British pleasure piers in existence. These piers are listed below, along with notable entertainment buildings and other interesting structures at resorts with and without piers; generally, lighthouses have not been included. Please note that mention in this list does not imply any form of public access, although many of these buildings are open to the public or visible from publicly accessible areas.

CHESHIRE
West Kirby: Column daymark (Column Road).

CORNWALL
Falmouth: National Maritime Museum. Fowey: Gribbin daymark (Gribbin Head). Penzance: Jubilee Pool, Egyptian House. St Ives: Tate St Ives.

CUMBRIA
Silloth: village.

DEVON
Exmouth: A la Ronde. Ilfracombe: Landmark Theatre. Lympstone: Peters Tower. Lynton: Cliff Railway. Paignton: Pier, Festival Hall, Torbay Cinema. Plymouth: Tinside Pool. Teignmouth: Pier. Torquay: Princess Pier, Pavilion.

DORSET
Boscombe: Pier. Bournemouth: Pier; Camera Obscura Café. Branksome: Solarium. Swanage: Pier. Weymouth: Commercial Pier and Pier Bandstand.

DURHAM
Whitburn, South Shields: Souter Lighthouse.

ESSEX
Burnham-on-Crouch: Royal Corinthian Yacht Club. Clacton: Pier. Harwich: Electric Palace Cinema. Southend-on-Sea: Pier, Kursaal, Observation Tower. Walton on the Naze: Pier.

HAMPSHIRE
Hythe: Pier. Southampton: Royal Pier. Southsea: Clarence and South Parade Piers.

ISLE OF WIGHT
Ryde: Pier, Pavilion. Sandown: Culver Pier. Totland Bay: Pier. Ventnor: Winter Gardens, waste-water treatment works. Yarmouth: Pier.

KENT
Deal: Pier. Dover: White Cliffs Centre. Gravesend: Pier, riverside café.
Herne Bay: Pier. Margate: Dreamland.

LANCASHIRE
Blackpool: Central, North and South Piers, Blackpool Tower, Winter
Gardens, Casino (Pleasure Beach), swivelling wind shelters. Fleetwood:
Pier, Radar Training Station. Morecambe: Victoria Pavilion, Midland Hotel.
St Anne's-on-the-Sea: Pier. Southport: Pier.

LINCOLNSHIRE
Cleethorpes: Pier. Ingoldmells: original chalet (now office), Butlin's
Holiday Camp. Mablethorpe: modern beach huts. Skegness: Pier.

NORFOLK
Cromer: Pier. Gorleston-on-Sea: Pavilion Theatre. Great Yarmouth:
Britannia and Wellington Piers, Hippodrome, Winter Gardens, Gem
(Windmill), Empire, Pleasure Beach.

NORTHUMBERLAND
Newbiggin by the Sea: sculpture *Couple* on breakwater. Tynemouth:
Railway (now Metro) Station, Life Brigade Watch House, former open air
baths. Whitley Bay: Spanish City.

SOMERSET
Burnham-on-Sea: Pier. Clevedon: Pier. Weston-super-Mare: Grand and
Birnbeck Piers, Knightstone Pavilion and Opera House.

SUFFOLK
Felixstowe: Pier. Lowestoft: Claremont and South Piers, East Point
Pavilion, Royal Norfolk and Suffolk Yacht Club, Ness Beacon. Southwold:
Pier. Thorpeness: village.

SUSSEX
Bexhill: De La Warr Pavilion, modern bandstand. Bognor Regis: Pier.
Brighton: Palace (Brighton) and West Piers, Royal Pavilion. Eastbourne:
Pier, waste-water treatment works. Hastings: Pier, Cliff Railway, net lofts,
White Rock Pavilion. Littlehampton: East Beach Café. Saltdean: Lido.
Worthing: Pier, Dome Cinema.

YORKSHIRE — EAST
Bridlington: South Promenade, Floral Hall.

YORKSHIRE — NORTH
Ravenscar: village. Saltburn: Pier, Cliff Lift. Scarborough: Grand Hotel, Cliff Lift, Northstead Manor Gardens, South Bay Pool, Spa Buildings.

ISLE OF MAN
Douglas: Camera Obscura, Gaiety Theatre, Villa Marina. Ramsey: Queen's Pier.

SCOTLAND
Dunoon: Queen's Hall. Rothesay: Winter Gardens, Pavilion, Pierhead Toilets. Wemyss Bay: Railway Station.

WALES
Aberystwyth: Royal Pier. Bangor: Bangor Garth Pier. Beaumaris: Pier. Colwyn Bay: Victoria Pier. Llandudno: Pier. Mumbles: Pier. Penarth: Pier. Portmeirion: village.

MUSEUMS
Beside the Seaside Museum, 34–35 Queen Street, Bridlington, East Yorkshire YO15 2SP. Telephone: 01262 608890.

Cromer Museum, East Cottages, Tucker Street, Cromer, Norfolk NR27 9HB. Telephone: 01263 513543. (Poppyland Gallery.) Website: www.museums.norfolk.gov.uk

North Down Heritage Centre, Town Hall, Bangor, County Down, Northern Ireland BT20 4BT. Telephone: 02891 271200. (Seaside Nostalgia Gallery.) Website: www.northdown.gov.uk/heritage/

North Somerset Museum, Burlington Street, Weston-super-Mare, Somerset BS23 1PR. Telephone: 01934 621028. (Seaside Holiday Gallery.) Website: www.n-somerset.gov.uk/Leisure/Museum/

Time and Tide Museum of Great Yarmouth Life, Blackfriars Road, Great Yarmouth, Norfolk NR30 3BX. Telephone: 01493 843930. Website: www.museums.norfolk.gov.uk

WEBSITES
Brighton West Pier Trust: www.westpier.co.uk
British Seaside History: www.seasidehistory.co.uk
Burnham-on-Sea Pier: www.burnham-on-sea.com/pier2.html
Clevedon Pier and Heritage Trust: www.clevedonpier.com
Coastal Treasures: www.coastaltreasures.eu
Colwyn Bay, Victoria Pier: www.victoriapier.com
Cromer Pier: www.cromer-pier.com
East Beach Café, Littlehampton (telephone: 01903 731903): www.eastbeachcafe.co.uk

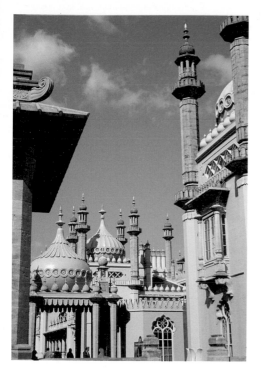

The Royal Pavilion, Brighton, is an extravagant Indian-style palace created in 1815–23 from the Marine Pavilion (1787) by the architect John Nash for George, Prince of Wales, who was first Prince Regent (1811–20), then King George IV (1820–30). The artist-designers Frederick Crace and Robert Jones produced the richly oriental interior decoration. The Pavilion was sold to Brighton by Queen Victoria in 1850.

Friends of Hastings Pier: www.friendsofhastingspier.com
Herne Bay Pier Trust: www.hernebaypier.com
Lidos in the United Kingdom: www.lidos.org.uk
National Piers Society: www.piers.co.uk
Slot machines on Southwold Pier: www.underthepier.com
Southwold Pier: www.southwoldpier.co.uk
Swanage Pier: www.swanagepiertrust.com
Victorian Society: www.victoriansociety.org.uk
Weston-super-Mare, Grand Pier: www.grandpierwsm.co.uk

Right: Cleethorpes Pier was built in 1872–3 for the Cleethorpes Promenade Pier Company; its original length was 1,200 feet. In 1884 the pier was taken on by the Manchester, Sheffield & Lincolnshire Railway Company, which added a pavilion in 1888, but this was burnt down in 1903. The pier is now 335 feet long as a result of breaching in 1940 and demolition after the war.

INDEX

Page numbers in italic refer to illustrations.

Aberystwyth Royal Pier 12, *12*, 62
Anderson, John 6, 40
Atelier One 49
Bangor Garth Pier *1*, 2, 14, *14*, 22, *24*, 62
Bauman Lyons 48
Bayes, Gilbert 27
Beach huts 17, 49, 51, *53*
Beaumaris Pier 62
Betjeman, Sir John 14
Bexhill, De La Warr Pavilion *38*, 39, 43–4, 45, 48, 61
Birch, Eugenius 7, 9, 10, 12, 16, 18, 19, 22
Birch, Peregrine 18
Blackpool 61: Alhambra 34; Casino 39, *40*, *45*, 46, 61; Central Pier *17*, 61; Derby Baths 44; Illuminations *39*, 40; North Pier 9, 10, 12, 16, *17*, 19, 50, 51, 61; Palace Pier 37, 39; Pleasure Beach 37, 39, 40, 45, 46, 61; South Pier 61; South Shore Promenade 49, *49*; Tower *17*, 31, 32, *33*, 34, 34, 37, *40*, 51, 61; Tower Ballroom 32, *33*; Tower Circus 32, 41; Winter Gardens 32, *33*, 34, 36, 37, 61
Bognor Regis Pier 14, 29, 61
Boscombe 51, 60
Boulton & Paul 14, 16
Bournemouth 60: Pier 12, 60; Winter Garden 31, 33
Branksome 60
Bridgman, George Soudon 46
Bridlington 54, 61: South Promenade Improvement Scheme 48, *48*, 51, *53*, 61
Brighton 5, 51, 61: Aquarium 12; Chain Pier 10; Palace Pier (Brighton Pier) 27, *28*, 61; Royal Pavilion 10, 61, *63*; Tower 49; West Pier 9, 10, 12, 18, *18*, 24, 27, 49, 61
Brown, Eric 23
Brunlees, Sir James 5, 12, 16, 36
Burmantofts 32, *34*, *41*
Burnham-on-Crouch, Royal Corinthian Yacht Club 41, *44*, 60
Burnham-on-Sea Pier 17, 61
Cackett & Burns Dick 36
Carrick, James 45
Carters of Poole 27, *52*
Chamberlin, Peter 23
Chermayeff, Serge 43
Chipperfield, David 49
Cinemas 18, 39, 40, *41*
Clacton Pier *15*, 60
Clarke, John 35
Clayton & Black 18
Cleethorpes 47–8, 61: Pier *15*, 61, *63*; Warwick's Revolving Tower 39
Clevedon Pier 8, 9, *10*, *11*, 22, 26, 61
Cliff railways 12, 39, *40*
Coade stone 27
Cockrill, J. W. 17, 18, 42
Cockrill, Ralph Scott 42
Cockrill, William 42
Colwyn Bay Victoria Pier *8*, *13*, 29, 62
Crescent Iron Works 19
Cromer Pier *15*, *20*, 21, 61
Crystal Palace 12, 31, 32
De Grineau, Bryan 23

Deal Pier 5, 9, 21, *22*, 49, 61
Dixon, John 5
Dorn, Marion 43
Douglas 62: Warwick's Revolving Tower 39
Doulton of Lambeth 27, *42*, *43*, *54*
Dover 61: Pier 14; White Cliffs Centre 48, 61
Dowson, J. E. 12
Dunoon Queen's Hall 47, 62
Eastbourne *54*, 61: Pier 12, *13*, 22, 61
Emberton, Joseph 41, 46
Emptage Architects 23
Exmouth, A la Ronde *52*, 60
Falmouth 60
Felixstowe 29, 61
Festival of Britain 21, 23, *23*, 47
Fleetwood 61: Pier 17, 61
Fowey, Gribbin daymark 51, 53, *53*, 60
Garrett, Henry Augustus 43
Gill, Eric 43
Gooding, Mel 48
Gorleston-on-Sea 61
Gravesend 6, 61
Great Yarmouth 61: Britannia Pier 2, *3*, 8, 16, 19, 37, 61; Empire Cinema *41*, 61; Gem (Windmill) Cinema 39, 41, *41*, 61; Hippodrome 41, *42*, 61; Warwick's Revolving Tower *37*, 39; Waterways 41; Wellington Pier 6, 7, 17, 18, *18*, 19, 31, 61; Winter Gardens 7, 18, *19*, 31, *33*, 61
Grover, John William 10
Halcrow, Sir William 21
Hamilton's Windsor Iron Works 10
Harvey, William 19
Harwich 60
Hastings 51, 61: Cliff Railway 39, 61; Pier 9, 11–12, *12*, *25*, 27, 29, 61; White Rock Pavilion 27, 61
Head Wrightson 12, 15
Heatherwick, Thomas 49
Henry, Sean 49
Heritage Lottery Fund 24, 25, 27
Herne Bay Pier 5, 7, 29, *29*, 61
Hewitt, Arthur S. 39, 41
Hill, Oliver 41
Hunstanton Pier 14
Hythe 60
Ilfracombe, Landmark Theatre 47, 48, 60
Ingoldmells 60
Johnston, Ninian 47
Jones, R. W. H. 46
Laidlaw, Robert 9, 17
Landmark Trust 52, 54
Latham, F. 45
Leith 5
Levitate Architecture and Design Studio 29
Lidos 45, 46, 55
Littlehampton, East Beach Café 49, *49*, 61
Llandudno Pier *4*, 5, 12, *13*, 16, *16*, 62
Lowestoft 11, 51, *53*, *54*, 61: Claremont Pier *17*, 29, 53, 61; East Point Pavilion *47*, 48, 61; Royal Norfolk and Suffolk Yacht

Club *47*, 61; South Pier 16, 21, 61
Lympstone, Peters Tower 54, 60
Lynton 60
Lytham 9
Mablethorpe 49, 61
MacFarlane, Walter 41, 43
Mangnall & Littlewoods 8, 16–17, 34
Margate 5, 61: Pier 7; Turner Contemporary 49
Marks Barfield 49
Marsh, W. Sutcliffe 56
Matcham, Frank 33, 34
Mathieson, Donald 28
Maxwell & Tuke 31, 32, 34
Mayoh, James and Arthur 2
Mayoh & Haley 2, 17, 18
McAslan, John 44
McChesney, Ian 49
McLaughlin, Niall 48–9
McLean, Bruce 48
Mendelsohn, Erich 43
Miller, James 28
Milton Iron Works 9, 11
Milton-on-Thames 6
Minehead Pier 14, 21
Moore, R. St George 27
Morecambe 61: Central Pier *16*, 19, *19*, 24; Midland Hotel 41, 43, 61; Tower *35*, 36; Warwick's Revolving Tower 39; West End Pier 8, 16, *17*, 19
Mumbles Pier 8, *56*, 62
National Piers Society 14, 21, 29, 59
National Trust 48, 52
New Brighton: Lido 46; Pier 10, 12; Tower 34–6, 34
Newbiggin by the Sea 49, 61
Nickols, Arthur 52
Noble Organization 28
Norton & Masey 32
Paignton 60: Festival Hall 46, 47, 60; Pier 46, 60
Penarth Pier 22, 56, 62
Penzance 60: Egyptian House *52*, 60; Jubilee Pool *45*, 46, 60
Pier railways 2, 10, 14, 25
Plymouth, Tinside Lido *55*, 60
Poole 27, 52
Portmeirion 51, 62
Ramsey Queen's Pier 29, 62
Ravenscar 62
Ravilious, Eric 13, 43
Read, R. J. G. 32
Redcar Pier 21–2
Rhyl: Pier 10, 12, 36; Queen's Palace 30, 31, 36, 37
Richardson, C. J. 31
Ridley, Noel 18
Robinson, John C. 46
Rogers, Edward 43
Ronalds, Tim 47
Rothesay 28, 31, 62: Pavilion 44, *45*, 62; Winter Gardens 41, *43*, 44, 62
Ryde 5, 60: Pavilion 41, 60; Pier 5, 6, 6, 60; Victoria Pier 6
St Anne's-on-the-Sea Pier 18, 61
St Ives, Tate St Ives 48, 60
St Leonards Palace Pier 21, 27
Saltburn 62: Cliff Railway 39, *40*, 62; Pier 6, 24–5, *26*, 40, 56, 62
Saltdean Lido 46, *46*, 61
Sandbanks *52*

Sandown *10*, 60
Saracen Foundry 41, 43
Scarborough 62: Aquarium 12; Cliff Railways 39, 40, 62; Grand Hotel 43, 62; Northstead Manor Gardens 41, 62; Pier 12; Warwick's Revolving Tower 39
Scheveningen 16
Shanklin Pier 24
Shaws of Darwen 33, 44
Shed KM 25
Sherrin, George 35
Sidmouth 51
Silloth 60
Skegness 61
Skipper, George 15, 47
Southampton Pier 5, 60
Southend-on-Sea 57, 60: Kursaal *35*, 36–7, 60; Pier 2, 5, 8, 12, *14*, *16*, *23*, 57, 60; Warwick's Revolving Tower 39
Southern Water 51, 54, 55
Southport 48, *48*, 57, 61: Pier 5, 6, 7–8, *8*, 12, 16, 24, *25*, 61; Winter Garden 31, 33
Southsea 60: Clarence Pier *15*, 60; South Parade Pier *15*, 60
Southwold *53*, 61: Pier *25*, *28*, 61
Spruce, E. Caldwell 34
Swanage 52, 60: Pier 22, 29, 60
Teignmouth Pier 14, 60
Thorpeness 51, 61
Thurley, C. F. J. 46
Torquay 60: Pavilion *43*, 60; Princess Pier 46, 60; Princess Theatre 46; Winter Gardens 18, 19, 31, *33*
Totland Bay 29, 60
Trainor, Michael 49
Truscon 45
Tynemouth 61: Winter Garden *32*
Urban Splash 29
Ventnor 51, *55*, 60: Royal Victoria Pier 24, 55; Winter Gardens 44, 55, 60
Walton-on-the-Naze Pier 5, 60
Ward, Richard J. 10
Warwick, Thomas 39
Warwick's Revolving Towers *37*, 39
Watson, John 19
Webster, John James 14
Wemyss Bay Station *38*, 62
West Kirby *57*, 60
Weston-super-Mare 61: Birnbeck Pier 9, 10, 12, 29, 61; Grand Pier *17*, *18*, 61
Westward Ho! Pier 14
Weymouth 5, 60: Pavilion Theatre 9
Whitburn 60
Whitley Bay 11, 61: Spanish City *36*, 61
Wibberley, J. S. 55
Widnes Foundry Company 8, 13, 17
Wilson, Joseph William 12, 14
Winter gardens 7, 16, 18, 19, 31, 32, 33, 34, 37, 41, 43, 44, 48
Worthing 61: Pier 19, 61
Wylson & Long 34
Yarmouth (IOW) 60